Tough times for adult learners

The NIACE survey on adult participation in learning 2011

Fiona Aldridge and Alan Tuckett

promoting adult learning

Published by the National Institute of Adult Continuing Education (England and Wales)

21 De Montfort Street

Leicester LE1 7GE

Company registration no. 2603322

Charity registration no. 1002775

http://www.niace.org.uk

Copyright © 2011 National Institute of Adult Continuing Education

(England and Wales)

NIACE, the national organisation for adult learning, has a broad remit to promote lifelong learning opportunities for adults. NIACE works to develop increased participation in education and training, particularly for those who do not have easy access because of barriers of class, gender, age, race, language and culture, learning difficulties and disabilities, or insufficient financial resources.

For details of all our publications, visit http://shop.niace.org.uk

Cataloguing in Publication Data

A CIP record of this title is available from the British Library

ISBN 978 1 86201 510 4

Designed and typeset by Book Production Services, London

Printed and bound in the UK

Contents

Acknowledgements

We are grateful for the support of the European Social Fund and the Local Government Association in the funding of this work; of our colleagues at TNS Omnibus who conducted the research; and of our colleagues at NIACE in the production of this report.

Introduction

The key message of the annual NIACE Survey on Adult Participation in Learning for 2011 is that recession is bad for lifelong learning for anyone over the age of 25. The survey highlights the central importance of workplaces as sites of adult learning – and the challenges posed to a learning society when opportunities to learn reduce. Far from the gap closing between the learning-rich and learning-poor, the report highlights the fact that professional and managerial groups are more than twice as likely to take part in learning as the least-skilled. Yet, only a year ago the lowest social class reported a sharp increase, suggesting that recent cutbacks in provision – whether public or private – have hurt most those who have had least benefit from their earlier experience of education and training. However, perhaps the most concerning aspect of the survey is the decline in reported future intentions to take up learning. Reductions in publicly funded provision, coupled with reduced workplace offers have, it seems, a depressing effect on people's expectations for themselves.

While the overall participation rate for current learners offers little cause for concern, having slipped by just one percentage point from 21 to 20, (which is well within the statistical margin of error), the total who have taken part in learning over the last three years has fallen from 43 per cent in 2010 to 39 per cent this year. These figures are particularly disappointing given the evidence in the 2010 survey both of increased participation, and of the numbers of people with a clear intention to take up learning over the next three years. The survey shows that the downward trend in men's participation (43 per cent in 1996 to just 37 per cent now) is continuing, with the 2011 survey showing the lowest percentage of men participating since the series began, reinforcing the popular perception that lifelong learning providers of all sorts are better at responding to women's needs than men's.

Changes in the balance of public investment in learning can be seen most clearly in the striking changes in opportunity and take-up reported by different age groups. Current participation among 17–19s has soared, showing a 13 percentage point gain on last year, (from 58 to 71 per cent) and a more modest gain of 4 percentage points is reported by 20–24s. Clearly the trend noted last year has continued and strengthened. In the uncertain conditions of an economic downturn, a larger proportion of young people respond by deciding to strengthen their skills and qualifications by staying in education, or taking work with training. The growth in apprenticeships over the last three years has helped here, too.

Meanwhile, for the bulk of the population of working age, opportunities have reduced and participation has dropped sharply, with current or recent participation amongst the 25–34s falling by 7 percentage points to 43 per cent (against 68 per cent among 20–24s). In part this can be explained by the decisions of successive governments to concentrate funding on 16–19s and to shift public subsidy for post-19s to the 19–24s at the expense of older learners. But publicly offered education and training only accounts for a proportion of the total, and a CIPD survey[1] indicating that more than 4 in 10 of their members have already cut back on training also contributes to the picture. Where companies do train, as report after report testifies, spending is concentrated on health and safety and induction training, and on senior managers.

Participation among 65–74s has also fallen, with current or recent participation down from 23 to 17 per cent, which means that over a quarter of learning opportunities for older adults has been lost, at a time when we know that learning has a positive impact on health, independence, and general well-being in later life – and when with an ageing labour force we need to encourage people to prolong their active working lives. Reducing learning opportunities will hardly help with the well-being or work-readiness of Britain's third-age adults.

In 2010 the survey showed the largest rise for a generation in participation amongst the least-skilled, with current or recent participation by social class DE rising to 30 per cent. This year just 23 per cent report current or recent study – the lowest rate recorded over 20 years. The rise and fall are both well outside the margins of statistical error, suggesting that confidence to take up learning amongst the least skilled was fragile and short-lived, but also that this group is the least likely to have its provision protected when economic circumstances change.

The importance of the workplace can be seen in the participation rates of workers, unemployed people and those outside the workforce. Among full-time employees there is a drop of 5 percentage points among current or recent participants – from 51 to 46 per cent, with slightly more of the fall concentrated among those offered training over the last three years. Almost the same volume and the same reduction are reported by part-time staff. People looking for work participate at nearly the same levels – with 41 per cent reporting current or recent study. For people outside the labour market and not looking for work, the picture is bleaker still with a 25 per cent participation rate, and only 15 per cent of retired people take part. The clear message here is that although opportunities at work are declining, it is still people in work who get most chances to learn.

That message is reinforced in a different part of the NIACE survey, where people were asked about motivation to learn and about the benefits of taking part. Asked whether the primary reason for taking up learning was for personal or leisure interests, or for work and career, 73 per cent of all learners reported a work-related motivation for taking part, with more than 80 per cent of those aged 17–54 agreeing. After that, unsurprisingly the pattern shifts. Among 55–64s there is still a majority (56 per cent), reporting work-related reasons, whilst 85 per cent of 65–74s are pursuing personal and leisure interests.

When it comes to benefits of learning the figures are even starker. When asked about the impact that learning as an adult can have on various aspects of life, 86 per cent of all adults agree that learning can have a positive impact on self confidence – a message consistently reported by adult learners in all kinds of settings. Eighty-three per cent also believe that learning as an adult can have positive effects on career and employment prospects, too. Seventy-five per cent acknowledge the positive effects on children's education, surely

---

1 CIPD (2011) *Learning and Development Talent Survey 2011*, CIPD. Available at **http://www.cipd.co.uk/hr-resources/survey-reports/learning-talent-development-2011.aspx**, accessed 27 April 2011.

reinforcing the argument that the inter-generational effects of lifelong learning are of great significance. A belief in the positive impact of adult learning on health (62 per cent) and on involvement in local issues and events (53 per cent) was also encouraging.

Perhaps the most dramatic change over the last decade has been the rise of the Internet as the first place of contact for anyone seeking information and advice about learning. Eight years ago the workplace dominated as a source of advice for everyone between the ages of 25 and 64. First came work, employer or training officer – cited by 20 per cent of all respondents in those age cohorts; next workmates, cited by 12 per cent. This year employer/work/training officer received between 3–8 per cent for 25–64s, and workmates just 1 per cent. There is a similar drop in people mentioning friends and family – from 12 per cent overall in 2002 to just 2 per cent now. The Internet, meanwhile, was cited by 43 per cent of all respondents, rising to 52 per cent for 25–34s. When this finding is linked to the pattern of participation in learning, where people with access to the Internet are well over twice as likely to participate as those without, it is clear that digital exclusion is increasingly acting to reinforce the marginalisation of those who are not connected.

However, the most curious finding of this survey was an increase in the numbers reporting no learning since school – up from 31 per cent to 39 per cent – well beyond sampling errors, which suggests that people have either forgotten passages of earlier learning (most likely perhaps where that learning is in informal settings or at work), or in line with an increased scepticism about the difference learning makes, a re-classification of whether activity previously seen as learning really counts. For a number of years Scottish respondents reported significantly lower levels of engagement than other people in the UK – challenging other data on provision in and out of work. Schuller and Field[2] suggested that this might be because Scots were more likely to count only more formal passages of learning in the self-reported study. We will need to explore whether a similar change is under way elsewhere in the UK, when we report on subsequent findings.

Key findings from the survey:

- One in five adults is currently engaged in some form of learning, with 39 per cent reporting participation in learning over the last three years. Since 2010, current participation has fallen from 21 to 20 per cent. Taking current and recent learning together, participation fell from 43 to 39 per cent (see Table 1).

- A greater proportion of women continue to participate in learning than men, although both report a fall of 4 percentage points against 2010. Male participation is now at its lowest level since the survey series began (see Figure 3).

- Socio-economic class remains a key predictor of adult participation in learning. Professional and managerial groups (ABs) are likely to participate at more than twice the rate of the least skilled and those outside the labour market (DEs). Since 2010, levels of participation among ABCs have decreased by 3–4 percentage points while participation among DEs has fallen by 7 percentage points to 23 per cent – the lowest reported total over 20 years (see Table 5).

2 Schuller, T. and Field, J. (1999) 'Is there a difference between initial and continuing education in Scotland and Northern Ireland?', *Scottish Journal of Adult and Continuing Education*, Vol. 5, No.2, pp 16–76.

- Adults outside the labour market have much lower levels of participation than those engaged in, or looking for, work. While opportunities to learn for both full- and part-time workers have declined, it remains true that people in work still have the greatest chance of taking part in learning (see Table 7).

- In general, the older people are, the less likely they are to participate in learning. Since 2010, participation in learning has increased among young adults aged 17–24, but has decreased across all other age groups. Among 17–19-year-olds in particular, current participation has soared from 58 to 71 per cent, with a more modest gain of 4 percentage points reported by those aged 20–24. At the other end of the age spectrum, the survey indicates a loss of over a quarter of learning opportunities for adults aged 65–74 (see Table 9).

- In previous surveys, terminal age of education has been a key predictor of participation in learning as an adult. The 2011 figures again confirm the key divide between those who leave school at the earliest opportunity and those who stay on for even a short while (see Table 11).

- White adults are significantly less likely than those from black and minority ethnic groups to have participated in learning during the past three years and are only half as likely to be currently learning. However, minority ethnic participation shows a drop of 6 percentage points against 2010, whilst the drop for white Britons is just 3 per cent (see Table 12).

- Well over one-fifth of respondents report no regular access to the Internet. Of these only 14 per cent report any current or recent learning, against 46 per cent of those with Internet access. The digital divide is certainly persistent (see Table 13).

- A third of current or recent learners (34 per cent) report this as the first learning they have done since leaving school. More than a quarter (29 per cent) are returning to learning after more than 3 years.

- Nearly three quarters (73 per cent) of current or recent learners said that they had enghaged in learning this for work or career reasons, including more than 80 per cent of respondents aged 17–54. Over 80 per cent of those aged 65 and over are learning for personal and leisure interests (see Figure 11).

- Twenty-eight per cent of learners are learning through work; 24 per cent through university or a higher education institute; 16 per cent through a further education, tertiary or sixth form college; 12 per cent independently; 7 per cent online; 6 per cent in adult education centres or the Workers' Education Association (WEA), and 8 per cent in other venues such as schools, voluntary or community organisations or health and leisure clubs.

- Thirty-seven per cent of adults who have left full-time education say that they are likely to take up learning in the next three years, against 47 per cent in 2010 (see Table 17).

- Data on future intentions to learn show that we can expect the learning divide to continue into the future, potentially becoming wider (see Table 22). Forty-eight per cent of ABs and 43 per cent of C1s say that they are likely to take up learning in the next three years, compared with 33 per cent of skilled manual workers (C2s) and 27 per cent of the least skilled and those dependent on benefits (DE).

- As with participation in learning, future intentions to learn tend to decline with age (see Table 26), particularly among adults aged 55 and over. Just 26 per cent of 55–64s, 13 per cent of 65–74s and 8 per cent of adults aged 75 and over are likely to take up learning in the next three years.

Taken together the survey findings pose challenges for public policy makers. Of course, judgments have to be made about what level of public investment is made directly in the creation of a learning-rich society. But government has more levers than simply paying for provision. The Leitch report,[3] published in 2006 promised a 2010 review of employers' patterns of investment in the development of their staff. But by the time 2010 came round the government of the day decided that review should be postponed until 2015. Meanwhile British industry and commerce invests less in its people than comparable OECD countries. In the light of the survey is it not time for government to revisit the case for licences to practise, as well as thinking how best to use its resources directly to encourage people to take part in learning?

---

3 HM Treasury (2006) *Leitch Review of Skills: Prosperity for All in the Global Economy – World Class Skills*, London, The Stationery Office.

Technical notes

This survey, undertaken for NIACE, as part of the TNS Omnibus, interviewed a weighted sample of 4,957 adults, aged 17 and over, in the UK in the period 16 February–6 March 2011. A range of questions was asked on adult participation in learning, with this report mainly concerned with the findings from the following two questions:

'Learning can mean practising, studying or reading about something. It can also mean being taught, instructed or coached. This is so you can develop skills, knowledge, abilities or understanding of something. Learning can also be called education or training. You can do it regularly (each day or month) or you can do it for a short period of time. It can be full time, or part time, done at home, at work, or in another place like a college. Learning does not have to lead to a qualification. We are interested in any learning you have done, whether or not it was finished.'

Which of the following statements most applies to you?
01: I am currently doing some learning activity
02: I have done some learning activity in the last three years
03: I have studied or learned but it was over three years ago
04: I have not studied or learned since I left full-time education
05: Don't know

How likely are you to take up learning in the next three years?
01: Very likely
02: Fairly likely
03: Fairly unlikely
04: Very unlikely
05: Don't know

Throughout this report percentages are rounded to the nearest whole number. Owing to this, and sensitivities introduced by weighting, some categories in the following tables may sum to slightly more than or less than 100 per cent. Further, any percentages calculated on small bases should be treated with caution as they may be subject to wide margins of sampling error. Tables are percentaged vertically unless otherwise specified. In tables, * indicates less than 0.5 per cent but greater than zero, and – indicates zero. NSR indicates not separately recorded and NA indicates not asked.

Participation in learning

The 2011 survey shows that one adult in five is currently engaged in some form of learning (20 per cent), with 39 per cent reporting participation in learning over the last three years (See Table 1 and Figure 1).

Although the overall participation rate for current learners has fallen by just one percentage point since 2010, the proportion who have taken part over the last three years has fallen from 43 to 39 per cent; returning to levels reported in 2009. These figures are particularly disappointing given the evidence in last year's survey of the increased numbers of adults with a clear intention to take up learning over the next three years.

Thirty-nine percent of adults say that they have not participated in any kind of learning since leaving full-time education. This figure is much higher than that reported in the 2010 survey – well beyond sampling error – suggesting that people have either forgotten earlier episodes of learning, or re-classified activity which they had previously counted as learning.

Table 1. Adult participation in learning – 1996, 1999, 2002, 2005, 2008, 2009, 2010 and 2011 compared

	1996 %	1999 %	2002 %	2005 %	2008 %	2009 %	2010 %	2011 %
Current learning	23	22	23	19	20	18	21	20
Recent learning (in the last three years)	17	18	19	22	19	21	22	18
All current or recent learning	**40**	**40**	**42**	**42**	**38**	**39**	**43**	**39**
Past learning (more than three years ago)	23	23	21	24	26	24	26	23
None since leaving full-time education/ don't know	36	37	36	35	36	37	31	39
Weighted base	4,755	5,205	5,885	5,053	5,033	4,917	4,964	4,967

Base: all respondents

Figure 1. Current or recent participation in learning, 1996–2011

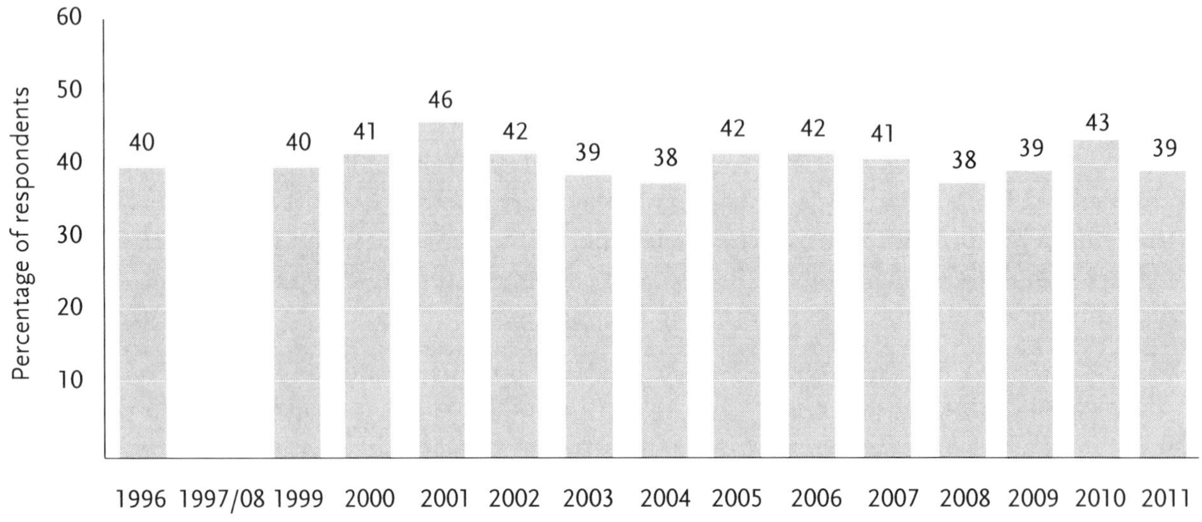

Base: all respondents

The definition of learning used within the NIACE series of surveys is deliberately broad and inclusive, being designed to capture a wide range of formal, non-formal and informal learning activity.

The learning reported in our survey extends far beyond publicly funded educational opportunities, although it has reflected the dramatic fall in the number of adult learners participating in publicly funded provision seen in recent years. Figures published by the Skills Funding Agency, in March 2011,[4] show a decrease in England of 6.1 per cent in the number of adult learners in 2009/10 compared to 2008/09, with around 1 million fewer adults now learning in publicly funded opportunities than was the case in 2004/05 (see Table 2). A similar pattern has been recorded in Wales, where figures published by the Welsh Assembly Government show a decrease in publicly funded education for adults of 3.44 per cent between 2008/09 and 2009/10.[5]

Table 2. Participation in courses funded by LSC/SFA, by learners aged 19+ (FE and skills participation – learner volumes), 2004/05 to 2009/10[a]

Learner numbers (percentage change from previous year in parentheses)

2004/05	2005/06	2006/07	2007/08	2008/09	2009/10
4,547,100	3,996,000 (−12.12%)	3,205,700 (−19.78%)	3,304,400 (+3.08%)	3,770,900 (+14.12%)	3,540,500 (−6.1%)

[a] Because of changes in the methodology in December 2008, learner numbers for 2008/09 onwards are not directly comparable with earlier years.

4 Data Service (2011) *Quarterly Statistical First Release: Post-16 Education & Skills: Learner Participation, Outcomes and Level of Highest Qualification Held* (DS/SFR10). http://www.thedataservice.org.uk/NR/rdonlyres/3AEFF9BC-8E53-41A1-8BCA-385DF0DB12D3/0/SFR_March11_Published.pdf
5 Welsh Assembly Government Lifelong Learning Wales Record (2010) *SDR 198/2010 Further Education, Work Based Learning, and Community Learning in Wales 2009-10 (provisional).* http://wales.gov.uk/docs/statistics/2010/101125sdr1982010en.pdf

The learning reported in our survey also extends beyond those opportunities that are directly related to the workplace, although levels of participation also reflect those reported by the Labour Force Survey which has shown declining levels of participation in job-related education and training since 2006 (see Figure 2). In quarter 1 of 2010, 25.6 per cent of employees reported participating in job-related education and training in the previous 13 weeks; slightly lower than that found in 2009.

Figure 2. Job-related education and training in the previous 13 weeks, England, Quarter 1

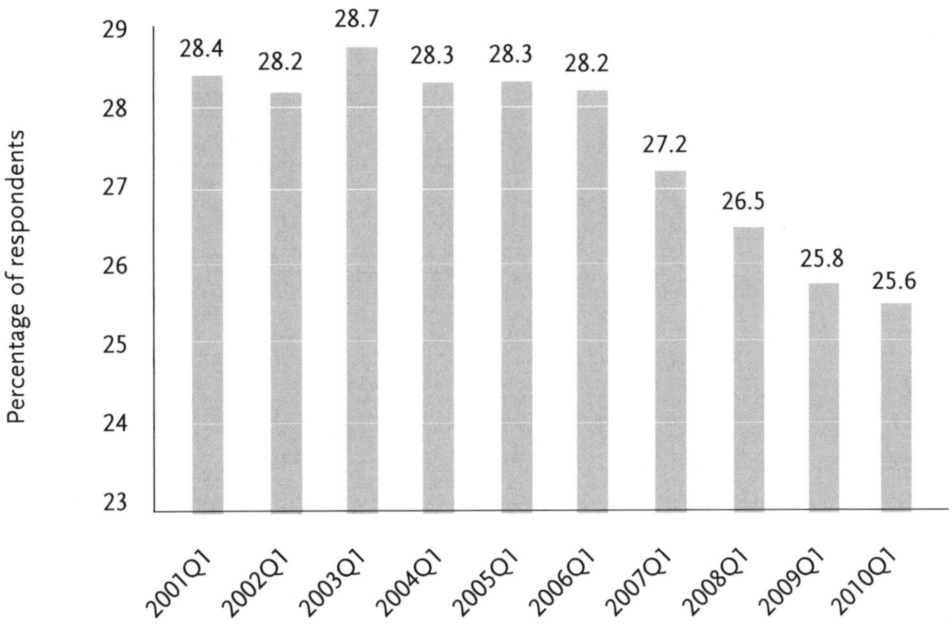

Source: Labour Force Survey, Q1 2001–2010

Participation in learning in relation to gender

NIACE's survey shows that women are more likely than men to have participated in learning during the past three years, although this difference is not significant among current learners. Equal proportions of men and women say that they have not participated in learning since leaving full-time education (see Table 3).

Table 3. Participation in learning 2011, men and women compared

	Total %	Men %	Women %
Current learning	20	19	21
Recent learning (in the last three years)	18	18	19
All current or recent learning	**39**	**37**	**40**
Past learning (more than three years ago)	23	23	22
None since leaving full-time education/ don't know	39	39	38
Weighted base	4,957	2,401	2,556

Base: all respondents

Since 2010, the proportion of both men and women participating in learning has decreased by 4 percentage points, such that male participation is now at its lowest level since the survey series began.

Since 1996, the gender gap has reversed and become narrower, with participation among men falling from 43 to 37 per cent, while female participation has increased from 38 to 40 per cent.

Figure 3. Current or recent participation in learning by gender, 1996–2011

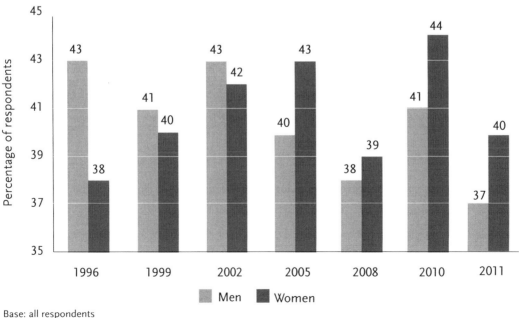

Base: all respondents

Participation in learning in relation to socio-economic class

Socio-economic class remains a key predictor of adult participation in learning (see Table 4). Fifty-two per cent of ABs and 48 per cent of C1s report taking part in learning during the past three years, compared with 34 per cent of skilled manual workers (C2s) and 23 per cent of unskilled workers and people on limited incomes (DEs).

Table 4. Participation in learning 2011, by socio-economic class[6]

	Total %	AB %	C1 %	C2 %	DE %
Current learning	20	27	29	14	12
Recent learning (in the last three years)	18	25	19	20	12
All current or recent learning	**39**	**52**	**48**	**34**	**23**
Past learning (more than three years ago)	23	26	24	24	19
None since leaving full-time education/ don't know	39	22	28	43	58
Weighted base	4,957	1,077	1,388	1,023	1,488

Base: all respondents

Since 2010, levels of participation among ABCs have decreased by 3–4 percentage points while participation among DEs has fallen by 7 percentage points to 23 per cent (see Table 5). Following the notable increase in levels of participation among DEs seen in the 2010 survey, it is disappointing that this has now fallen back to the lowest seen since the survey series began (see Figure 4), especially given 2010's report of rising expectations of future participation.

6 Social Grade A includes the upper and upper-middle classes and is generally grouped with Grade B, the middle classes. Grade C1 includes the lower-middle class, often called white-collar workers. Grade C2 mainly consists of skilled manual workers. Grade D comprises the semi-skilled and unskilled working class, and is usually linked with Grade E, those on the lowest levels of subsistence such as old age pensioners and those dependent upon welfare benefits.

Figure 4. Proportion of DEs who are not engaged in learning, 1996–2011

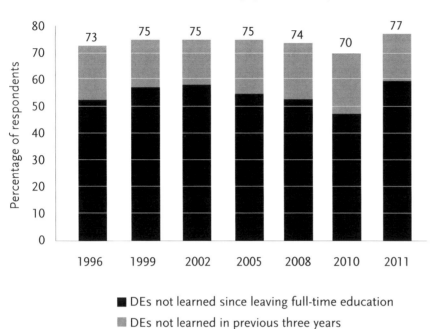

Base: all respondents in socio-economic group DE

As a result, ABC1s remain almost twice as likely to participate in learning as DEs. Nearly three-fifths (58 per cent) of this latter group have yet to take part in any form of learning activity since leaving school, while over three-quarters (77 per cent) of them have not engaged in learning in the previous three years (see Figure 5).

Figure 5. Proportion of adults who are not engaged in learning, by socio-economic class, 2011

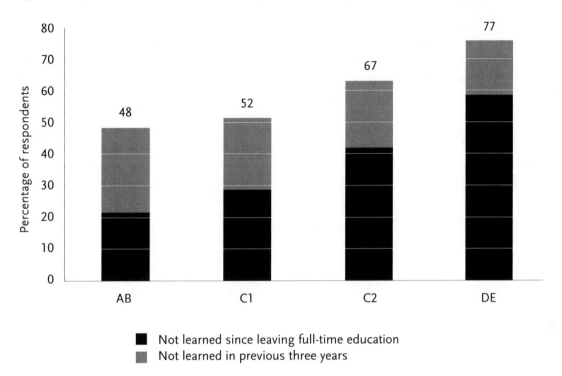

Not learned since leaving full-time education
Not learned in previous three years

Base: all respondents

Looking across the series, levels of participation in learning have decreased or remained broadly constant across all socio-economic groups (see Table 5).

Table 5. Current or recent participation in learning by socio-economic class – 1996, 1999, 2002 2005, 2008, 2010 and 2011 compared

	1996 %	1999 %	2002 %	2005 %	2008 %	2010 %	2011 %
Total sample	40	40	42	42	38	43	39
AB	53	58	60	56	51	56	52
C1	52	51	54	51	46	51	48
C2	33	36	37	40	33	37	34
DE	26	24	25	26	26	30	23
Weighted base	4,755	5,205	5,885	5,053	4,932	4,964	4,957

Base: all respondents

Participation in learning in relation to employment status

The importance of the workplace can be seen in the participation rates of workers, unemployed people and those outside the workforce. Just under one-half of full-time (46 per cent) and part-time workers (45 per cent) and 41 per cent of unemployed adults report current or recent participation in learning compared with 25 per cent of those who are not working and 15 per cent of retired adults (see Table 6).

Over one-half of those who are retired or not working say that they have not been involved in any learning since leaving full-time education, compared with one-third of adults who are working full or part time, and 38 per cent of those who are registered as being unemployed.

Table 6. Participation in learning 2011, by employment status

	Total %	Full time %	Part time %	Unemployed[7] %	Not working %	Retired %
Current learning	20	20	21	13	11	7
Recent learning	18	26	23	28	14	8
All current or recent learning	**39**	**46**	**45**	**41**	**25**	**15**
Past learning	23	22	23	21	24	28
None since leaving full-time education/don't know	39	32	32	38	50	56
Weighted base	4,957	1,941	615	301	525	1,264

Base: all respondents

Since 2010, levels of participation in learning have decreased across all groups, with the smallest decline seen among unemployed adults. Participation by retired adults has fallen by one-quarter over the previous 12 months, and by one-sixth among other adults who are not working (see Table 7). The clear message here is that whilst opportunities at work are declining it is still people in work who get most opportunity to learn (see Figure 6).

---

7 Includes only those who are registered as unemployed and claiming JSA.

Table 7. Current or recent participation in learning by employment status – 1996, 1999, 2002, 2005, 2008, 2010 and 2011 compared

	1996 %	1999 %	2002 %	2005 %	2008 %	2010 %	2011 %
Total sample	40	40	42	42	38	43	39
Full-time employment	49	51	52	52	45	51	46
Part-time employment	42	50	51	53	48	50	45
Unemployed	40	41	46	40	43	43	41
Not working	23	30	31	30	26	30	25
Retired	20	16	19	17	17	20	15
Weighted base	4,755	5,205	5,885	5,053	4,932	4,964	4,957

Base: all respondents

Figure 6. Proportion of adults who are not engaged in learning, by employment status, 2011

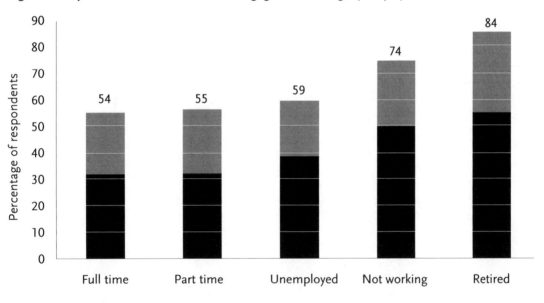

Base: all respondents

Participation in learning in relation to age

In general, the older people are, the less likely they are to participate in learning (see Table 8 and Figure 7). Eighty-eight per cent of 17–19-year-olds and 68 per cent of 20–24-year-olds are current or recent learners, compared with around two-fifths of the rest of the working-age population. The decline in participation is particularly steep for those aged 55 and over, such that only 29 per cent of adults aged 55–64, 17 per cent of adults aged 65–74 and 11 per cent of those aged 75 and over regard themselves as learners.

Table 8. Participation in learning 2011, by age

	Total %	17–19 %	20–24 %	25–34 %	35–44 %	45–54 %	55–64 %	65–74 %	75+ %
Current learning	20	71	44	23	18	18	11	9	6
Recent learning	18	16	24	20	23	23	18	8	5
All current or recent learning	**39**	**88**	**68**	**43**	**42**	**41**	**29**	**17**	**11**
Past learning	23	9	21	36	36	33	40	54	62
None since leaving full-time education/ don't know	39	10	23	37	36	34	41	54	62
Weighted base	4,957	207	454	906	851	778	792	511	458

Base: all respondents

Figure 7. Proportion of adults who are not engaged in learning, by age, 2011

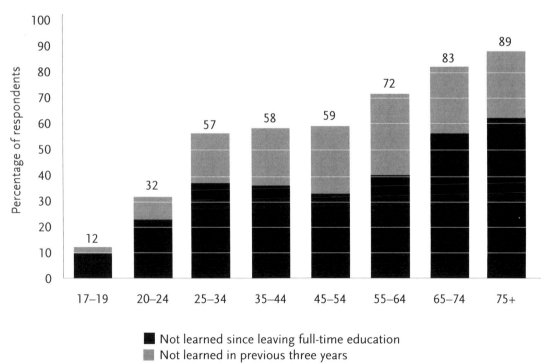

Base: all respondents

Since 2010, participation in learning has increased among young adults aged 17–24, but has decreased across all other age groups, with the most notable falls being among those aged 25–34 (7 percentage points) and those aged 65 and over.

Among 17–19-year-olds in particular, current participation has soared from 58 to 71 per cent, with a more modest gain of 4 percentage points reported by those aged 20–24. At the other end of the age spectrum, current or recent participation among those aged 65–74 has fallen from 23 to 17 per cent, representing a loss of over a quarter of learning opportunities for this adults in this age group.

Table 9 shows in parentheses the proportion of each age group in full-time education. Overall, as in 2010, 7 per cent of all respondents are in full-time education. However in 2011, this is comprised of a much higher proportion of young people aged 17–19 (+10 percentage points) and 20–24 (+6 percentage points), with fewer full-time students aged 25 and over.

Table 9. Current or recent participation in learning by age – 1996, 1999, 2002, 2005, 2008, 2010 and 2011 compared

	1996 %	1999 %	2002 %	2005 %	2008 %	2010 %	2011 %
Total sample	40 (5)[a]	40 (4)	42 (4)	42 (5)	38 (5)	43 (7)	39 (7)
17–19	86 (42)	81 (37)	78 (34)	75 (46)	79 (52)	85 (55)	88 (65)
20–24	65 (15)	70 (25)	72 (27)	63 (29)	60 (22)	66 (26)	68 (32)
25–34	48 (2)	50 (2)	51 (2)	52 (4)	43 (2)	50 (7)	43 (5)
35–44	43 (1)	47 (1)	47 (2)	49 (1)	46 (1)	45 (2)	42 (1)
45–54	36 (1)	41 (*)	44 (1)	47 (*)	40 (*)	44 (1)	41 (*)
55–64	25 (*)	29 (–)	30 (–)	32 (–)	29 (*)	33 (*)	29 (–)
65–74	19 (2)	16 (–)	20 (–)	17 (–)	19 (*)	23 (–)	17 (–)
75+	15 (–)	9 (–)	10 (–)	10 (–)	11 (–)	14 (–)	11 (–)
Weighted base	4,755	5,205	5,885	5,053	4,932	4,964	4,957

Base: all respondents

a Figures in parentheses show the proportion of each age group in full-time education

In 2009, NIACE published *Learning Through Life*, the final report of the independent Inquiry into the Future for Lifelong Learning.[8] One of the principal recommendations of the Inquiry was to base lifelong learning policy on a four-stage model (under 25, 25–49, 50–74, 75+) as a basis for a coherent systematic approach to lifelong learning. One of the key implications of this restructuring would be being a revision of the collection and analysis of public data on education and training to be consistent with this structure.

8 Schuller, T. and Watson, D. (2009) *Learning Through Life: Inquiry into the Future for Lifelong Learning (IFLL)*, Leicester: NIACE.

Table 10 provides a look at what information such an analysis might provide. Nearly three-quarters of young adults under 25 have taken part in learning during the previous 3 years, compared with 42 per cent of those aged 25–49, 28 per cent of those aged 50–74 and just 11 per cent of those aged 75 and over.

Since 2010, when figures were first presented in this way, the proportion of 17–24-year-olds learning in the previous 3 years has fallen by just one percentage point, though current participation has risen by 2 percentage points. Current or recent participation among adults in the other three stages has fallen by 6, 4 and 3 percentage points respectively.

Table 10. Participation in learning across the four stages, 2011

	Total %	18–24 %	25–49 %	50–74 %	75+ %
Current learning	20	49	20	12	6
Recent learning (in the last three years)	18	23	22	16	5
All current or recent learning	**39**	**72**	**42**	**28**	**11**
Past learning (more than three years ago)	23	8	22	28	27
None since leaving full-time education/ don't know	39	20	36	44	62
Weighted base	4,957	596	2,154	1,683	458

Base: all respondents

Participation in learning in relation to terminal age of education

In previous surveys, terminal age of education has been a key predictor of participation in learning as an adult. The 2011 figures again confirm the key divide between those who leave school at the earliest opportunity and those who stay on for even a short while (see Table 11 and Figure 8). Fifty per cent of people staying on in initial education to 21 or more report current or recent learning, compared with 24 per cent of those who left school aged 16 or younger.

Table 11. Participation in learning 2011, by terminal age of education

	Total %	Up to 16 %	17–18 %	19–20 %	21+ %
Current learning	20	10	17	15	24
Recent learning (in the last three years)	18	15	25	23	26
All current or recent learning	**39**	**24**	**42**	**38**	**50**
Past learning (more than three years ago)	23	23	26	25	25
None since leaving full-time education/ don't know	39	52	33	38	25
Weighted base	4,957	2,319	875	352	1,041

Base: all respondents

Figure 8. Proportion of adults who are not engaged in learning, by terminal age of education, 2011

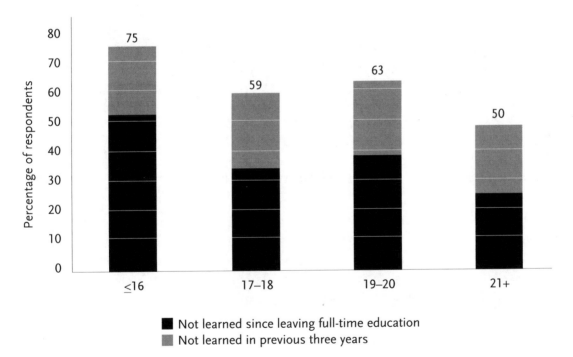

Base: all respondents

Participation in learning in relation to ethnicity

The survey shows that white respondents (38 per cent) are significantly less likely than black and minority ethnic adults (48 per cent) to have participated in learning during the past three years (see Table 12) and are only half as likely to be currently learning.

The size of the sample precludes us from disaggregating overall findings for distinct minority groups, although our analysis of Labour Force Survey data on participation in learning by ethnicity indicates that there are often dramatic differences in levels of participation between particular groups and subgroups of minority ethnic adults.[9]

Table 12. Participation in learning 2011, white and minority ethnic compared

	Total %	White %	Minority Ethnic %
Current learning	20	18	35
Recent learning (in the last three years)	18	19	13
All current or recent learning	**39**	**38**	**48**
Past learning (more than three years ago)	23	24	13
None since leaving full-time education/don't know	39	39	38
Weighted base	4,957	4,401	537

Base: all respondents

Participation in learning in relation to Internet access

Data on access to the Internet highlight that the digital divide continues to reinforce the learning divide (see Table 13). Only 14 per cent of those without access to the Internet report current or recent participation in learning, compared with 46 per cent of those with Internet access. As Internet access increases, the divide between those who have access and those without is likely to widen even further.

9 Aldridge, F., Lamb, H. and Tuckett, A. (2008) *Are We Closing the Gap? A NIACE Briefing on Participation in Learning by Adults from Minority Ethnic Groups,* Leicester: NIACE.

Table 13. Participation in learning 2011, by access to the Internet

	Total %	No Internet access %	Any Internet access %
Current learning	20	5	25
Recent learning (in the last three years)	18	9	21
All current or recent learning	**39**	**14**	**46**
Past learning (more than three years ago)	23	21	23
None since leaving full-time education/ don't know	39	65	31
Weighted base	4,957	1,186	3,862

Base: all respondents

Participation in learning and future intentions to learn in relation to nations of the UK and English regions

The 2011 data shows no significant variation in levels of participation or future intentions to learn between adults in any of the four UK nations (see Tables 14 and 16). Adults in Northern Ireland are most likely to report engagement in learning, although the small sample size should be noted.

Little variation also exists in participation in learning or future intentions to learn between the English regions, with only adults in Yorkshire and Humberside and the South West significantly more likely to be learning (see Table 16).

Table 14. Participation in learning 2011, by nation of the UK

	Total %	England %	Wales %	Scotland %	Northern Ireland %
Current learning	20	20	19	21	18
Recent learning (in the last three years)	18	18	20	17	27
All current or recent learning	**39**	**38**	**39**	**39**	**45**
Past learning (more than three years ago)	23	23	24	23	20
None since leaving full-time education/ don't know	39	39	38	36	35
Weighted base	4,957	4,164	247	394	152

Base: all respondents

It is necessary to remember the smaller sample sizes involved when examining data concerning Wales, Scotland and particularly Northern Ireland, which should be interpreted with care.

Since 2010, levels of adult participation in learning have increased slightly in Scotland and decreased elsewhere (see Table 15).

Table 15. Current or recent participation in learning by nation of the UK – 1996, 1999, 2002, 2005, 2008, 2010 and 2011 compared

	1996	1999	2002	2005	2008	2010	2011
	%	%	%	%	%	%	%
Total sample	40	40	42	42	38	43	39
England	42	41	42	42	39	43	38
Wales	37	43	39	42	38	46	39
Scotland	38	33	44	36	31	38	39
Northern Ireland	28	32	40	37	40	54	45
Weighted base	4,755	5,205	5,885	5,053	4,932	4,964	4,957

Base: all respondents

Table 16. Participation in learning and future intentions to learn 2011, by nations of the UK and English government office regions

	Weighted base	Current or recent participation[a]		Future intentions[b]	
		2011 %	Change since 2010 % (percentage points)	Total likely %	Total unlikely %
Total: United Kingdom	4,957	39	−4	37	60
South West	426	44	+3	38	59
Yorkshire & Humberside	352	42	−2	41	58
West Midlands	436	40	+1	37	61
East Midlands	352	40	0	32	65
North East	225	39	−5	40	58
South East	680	38	−4	35	62
London	610	37	−13	36	62
North West	565	35	−8	35	62
East of England	460	34	−5	38	61
Northern Ireland	152	54	−9	42	54
Wales	247	39	−7	39	57
Scotland	394	39	+1	40	57
England	4,164	38	−5	37	61

Base: a all respondents; b all respondents who have finished full-time education. Percentages are horizontal

Over the series, NIACE surveys have reported regional and national participation rates that have fluctuated widely. The smaller levels of variation found in recent surveys may in part be as a result of a stronger commitment to regional planning. However, the 2011 change in participation in London, which shows a drop of a quarter in the proportion participating is exceptional.

Future intentions to learn

In 2011, 37 per cent of adults who have left full-time education say that they are likely to take up learning in the next three years, while 60 per cent say that they are unlikely to do so (see Table 17).

Since the 2010 survey, future intentions to learn among adults who have left full-time education have decreased significantly by 10 percentage points, to the level found in 2009. As striking is the 11 point increase – from 34 per cent in 2010 to 45 per cent in 2011 – who say that they are *very* unlikely to take up learning in the next three years.

Table 17. Future intentions to take up learning,[10] 2002 to 2011 compared

	2002 %	2003 %	2004 %	2005 %	2006 %	2007 %	2008 %	2009 %	2010 %	2011 %
Very likely	20	19	21	19	22	25	19	19	24	19
Fairly likely	19	20	18	20	22	18	17	19	23	18
Total likely	**39**	**39**	**39**	**39**	**45**	**43**	**36**	**37**	**47**	**37**
Fairly unlikely	10	14	12	13	14	12	14	12	16	16
Very unlikely	48	44	47	45	38	43	46	47	34	45
Total unlikely	**58**	**58**	**59**	**57**	**52**	**55**	**61**	**59**	**50**	**60**
Don't know	3	3	3	4	3	2	3	3	3	3
Weighted base	4,688	4,658	4,644	4,816	4,690	4,669	4,691	4,680	4,705	4,616

Base: all respondents who have finished full-time education

Future intentions to learn in relation to learning status

The 2011 survey reinforces findings from previous years, which suggest that current participation has a significant impact upon future intentions to learn (see Table 18 and Figure 9).

Eighty per cent of current learners report that they are likely to take up learning in the future, compared with only 14 per cent of those who have not participated since leaving full-time education. Over four-fifths (84 per cent) of those who have not participated in learning since leaving full-time education say that they have no intention of doing so in the future.

---

10 In some years this question has been asked of all respondents. In 2005 and 2008 it was asked of all respondents who had left full-time education. Because of the electronic availability of data from 2002 onwards, it has been possible to recalculate the figures for these years. Data on future intentions to learn since 1996 are available in previous NIACE publications or on request.

Table 18. Future intentions to take up learning 2011, by learning status

	Total %	Current learners %	Recent learners %	Past learners %	Not since leaving full-time education %
Very likely	19	60	32	8	5
Fairly likely	18	20	33	21	9
Total likely	**37**	**80**	**65**	**28**	**14**
Fairly unlikely	16	9	14	22	15
Very unlikely	45	9	18	47	70
Total unlikely	**60**	**18**	**32**	**70**	**84**
Don't know	3	3	3	2	2
Weighted base	4,616	681	906	1,124	1,876

Base: all respondents who have finished full-time education

Figure 9. Future intentions to learn by learning status, 2011

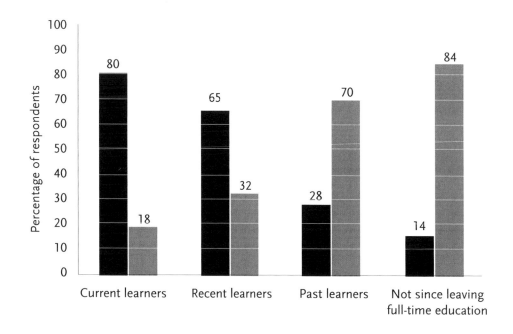

Base: all respondents who have finished full-time education

Future intentions to learn in relation to gender

Forty per cent of women and 34 per cent of men who have left full-time education report that they are likely to take up learning in the future. Nearly one-half of men (47 per cent) and 43 per cent of women say that they are *very* unlikely to take up learning in the next three years (see Table 19).

Table 19. Future intentions to take up learning 2011, by gender

	Total %	Men %	Women %
Very likely	19	17	21
Fairly likely	18	17	19
Total likely	**37**	**34**	**40**
Fairly unlikely	16	17	15
Very unlikely	45	47	43
Total unlikely	**60**	**64**	**58**
Don't know	3	3	2
Weighted base	4,616	2,245	2,370

Base: all respondents who have finished full-time education

Since 2010, levels of future intention to learn have fallen 12 points, from 46 to 34 per cent, among men and 8 points, from 48 to 40 per cent, among women (see Table 20).

Table 20. 'Likely to learn in the next three years' by gender, 2005–2011 compared

	2005 %	2006 %	2007 %	2008 %	2009 %	2010 %	2011 %
Total	39	45	43	36	39	47	37
Men	38	43	42	33	36	46	34
Women	40	47	45	39	39	48	40
Weighted base	4,816	4,690	4,669	4,691	4,680	4,705	4,616

Base: all respondents who have finished full-time education

Future intentions to learn in relation to socio-economic class

Data on future intentions to learn also show that we can expect the learning divide to continue into the future, potentially becoming wider (see Table 21). Forty-eight per cent of ABs and 43 per cent of C1s say that they are likely to take up learning in the next three years, compared with 33 per cent of skilled manual workers (C2s) and 27 per cent of the least skilled and those dependent on benefits (DE).

Table 21. Future intentions to take up learning 2010, by socio-economic class[11]

	Total %	AB %	C1 %	C2 %	DE %
Very likely	19	27	22	18	11
Fairly likely	18	21	21	15	16
Total likely	**37**	**48**	**43**	**33**	**27**
Fairly unlikely	16	17	19	16	11
Very unlikely	45	34	37	48	58
Total unlikely	**60**	**51**	**55**	**64**	**69**
Don't know	3	1	2	3	3
Weighted base	4,616	1,027	1,199	981	1,409

Base: all respondents who have finished full-time education

Since 2010, levels of future intention to learn have decreased across all socio-economic groups (see Table 22), with the largest decrease seen among C2s (–13 percentage points) and the smallest decrease among DEs (–8 percentage points).

Table 22. 'Likely to learn in the next three years' by socio-economic class, 2005–2011 compared

	2005 %	2006 %	2007 %	2008 %	2009 %	2010 %	2011 %
Total	39	45	43	36	37	47	37
AB	50	58	56	45	47	58	48
C1	46	52	48	40	46	54	43
C2	39	44	42	34	30	46	33
DE	26	31	32	28	27	35	27
Weighted base	4,816	4,690	4,669	4,691	4,680	4,705	4,616

Base: all respondents who have finished full-time education

11 Grade A includes the upper and upper-middle classes and is generally grouped with Grade B, the middle classes. Grade C1 includes the lower-middle class, often called white-collar workers. Grade C2 mainly consists of skilled manual workers. Grade D comprises the semi-skilled and unskilled working class, and is usually linked with Grade E, those on the lowest levels of subsistence such as old age pensioners and those dependent upon welfare benefits.

Future intentions to learn in relation to employment status

Employment status also has some impact upon future intentions to learn (see Table 23). Around one half of full-time workers (47 per cent), part-time (46 per cent) workers and unemployed adults (52 per cent), say that they are likely to take up learning in the future, compared with 41 per cent of those who are not working, but only 12 per cent of retired adults.

Table 23. Future intentions to take up learning 2011, by employment status

	Total %	Full-time %	Part-time %	Unemployed %	Not working %	Retired %
Very likely	19	25	23	21	20	5
Fairly likely	18	21	23	31	21	7
Total likely	**37**	**47**	**46**	**52**	**41**	**12**
Fairly unlikely	16	19	17	16	14	10
Very unlikely	45	32	35	19	42	76
Total unlikely	**60**	**51**	**51**	**45**	**56**	**86**
Don't know	3	3	3	3	3	2
Weighted base	4,616	1,927	579	295	518	1,263

Base: all respondents who have finished full-time education

Since 2010, levels of future intention to learn have decreased across all categories of employment status, with the most pronounced decreases among the unemployed (–15 percentage points), full-time workers (–13 percentage points) and part-time workers (–12 percentage points).

Although levels of future intentions to learn are generally lower among retired adults and those who are not working, they have been less affected by this year's overall decline (Table 24).

Table 24. 'Likely to learn in the next three years' by employment status, 2005–2011 compared

	2005 %	2006 %	2007 %	2008 %	2009 %	2010 %	2011 %
Total	39	45	43	36	37	47	37
Full time	52	57	55	46	47	60	47
Part time	50	57	54	46	49	58	46
Unemployed	49	60	56	47	50	67	52
Not working	37	44	43	37	40	44	41
Retired	12	16	17	12	11	17	12
Weighted base	4,816	4,690	4,669	4,691	4,680	4,705	4,616

Base: all respondents who have finished full-time education

Future intentions to learn in relation to age

As with participation in learning, future intentions to learn tend to decline with age (see Table 25 and Figure 10), particularly among adults aged 55 and over.

Table 25. Future intentions to take up learning 2011, by age

	Total %	17–19 %	20–24 %	25–34 %	35–44 %	45–54 %	55–64 %	65–74 %	75+ %
Very likely	19	40	28	26	26	24	12	5	4
Fairly likely	18	22	31	25	23	20	14	8	4
Total likely	**37**	**62**	**58**	**51**	**48**	**44**	**26**	**13**	**8**
Fairly unlikely	16	12	14	18	18	18	16	10	9
Very unlikely	45	23	26	28	31	36	55	75	83
Total unlikely	**60**	**36**	**40**	**46**	**49**	**54**	**71**	**85**	**91**
Don't know	3	3	2	3	3	2	3	2	1
Weighted base	4,616	73	308	857	840	776	792	511	457

Base: all respondents who have finished full-time education

Figure 10. Future intentions to learn by age, 2011

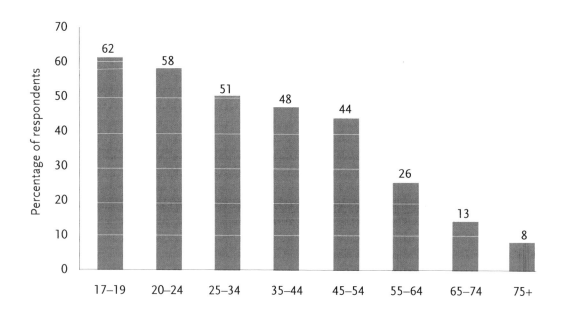

Base: all respondents who have finished full-time education

Table 26 shows future intentions to learn, by age, using the four-stage model as proposed in *Learning Through Life.*[12] Fifty-eight per cent of 18–24-year-olds say that they are likely to take up learning in the next three years, compared with one-half (49 per cent) of those aged 25–49, one quarter (26 per cent) of those aged 50–74 and just 8 per cent of those aged 75+.

Since 2010, when figures were first presented in this way, future intentions to learn among 25–49-year-olds have fallen 2 percentage points, while falling 6 percentage points across the other three stages.

Table 26. Future intentions to take up learning 2011, by life stages

	Total %	18–24 %	25–49 %	50–74 %	75+ %
Very likely	19	29	26	12	4
Fairly likely	18	29	23	14	4
Total likely	**37**	**58**	**49**	**26**	**8**
Fairly unlikely	16	14	18	14	9
Very unlikely	45	26	30	58	83
Total unlikely	**60**	**40**	**48**	**72**	**91**
Don't know	3	2	3	2	1
Weighted base	4,616	367	2,093	1,692	457

Base: all respondents who have finished full-time education

Since 2010 levels of future intention to learn have decreased across all age categories, with the sharpest decreases among those aged 35 and under (see Table 27).

Table 27. 'Likely to learn in the next three years' by age, 2005–2011 compared

	2005 %	2006 %	2007 %	2008 %	2009 %	2010 %	2011 %
Total	39	45	43	36	37	47	37
17–19	56	76	59	61	61	78	62
20–24	55	65	63	58	62	74	58
25–34	58	64	59	53	55	65	51
35–44	52	56	55	48	52	59	48
45–54	45	47	51	37	44	52	44
55–64	27	34	33	24	25	34	26
65–74	11	17	18	12	12	20	13
75+	4	7	10	8	7	10	8
Weighted base	4,816	4,690	4,669	4,691	4,680	4,705	4,616

Base: all respondents who have finished full-time education

12 Schuller, T. and Watson, D. (2009) *Learning Through Life: Inquiry into the Future for Lifelong Learning (IFLL)*, Leicester: NIACE.

Future intentions to learn in relation to ethnicity

Forty-four per cent of black and minority ethnic adults say that they are likely to take up learning in the next three years compared with 37 per cent of white adults (see Table 28).

Similar proportions of white (45 per cent) and black and minority ethnic (43 per cent) adults say that they are *very* unlikely to learn in the future.

Table 28. Future intentions to take up learning 2011, by ethnicity

	Total %	White %	Minority ethnic %
Very likely	19	18	26
Fairly likely	18	18	18
Total likely	**37**	**37**	**44**
Fairly unlikely	16	16	11
Very unlikely	45	45	43
Total unlikely	**60**	**61**	**54**
Don't know	3	3	2
Weighted base	4,616	4,179	418

Base: all respondents who have finished full-time education

Future intentions to learn in relation to Internet access

Sixteen per cent of those without Internet access say that they are likely to take up learning in the next three years compared with 44 per cent of those with access (see Table 29).

The learning divide between those who have access to the Internet and those without has widened in recent years and looks likely to continue to do so. Those without access are twice as likely as those with Internet access to say that they are *very* unlikely to take up learning in the next three years.

Table 29. Future intentions to take up learning 2011, by access to the Internet

	Total %	Any Internet access %	No Internet access %
Very likely	19	23	6
Fairly likely	18	21	10
Total likely	**37**	**44**	**16**
Fairly unlikely	16	17	10
Very unlikely	45	37	72
Total unlikely	**60**	**54**	**82**
Don't know	3	3	3
Weighted base	4,616	3,529	1,087

Base: all respondents who have finished full-time education

Motivation for learning and the benefits of taking part

When asked about why they had taken up learning, nearly three-quarters (73 per cent) of current or recent learners said that they had done this for work or career reasons, while the remaining quarter (26 per cent) were learning for leisure or personal interest. Women were significantly more likely to be learning for leisure or personal interest, as were those aged over 55 (see Figure 11), and DEs, i.e. unskilled workers and those on limited incomes.

Figure 11. Reasons for taking up learning, by age, 2011

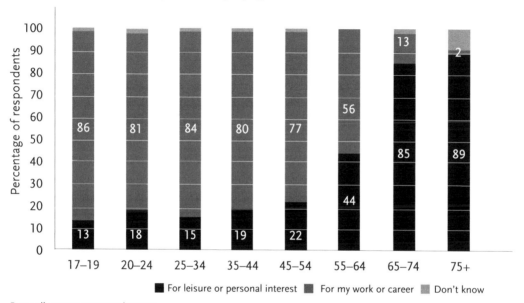

Base: all current or recent learners

All respondents, including those not engaged in learning were questioned about the extent to which they thought learning as an adult can have an impact on various aspects of life. Eighty-six per cent of adults believe that learning as an adult has a positive impact on self confidence; 83 per cent on career and employment prospects; 75 per cent on your children's education; 62 per cent on your health; 61 per cent on family relationships and 53 per cent on involvement in local events and issues.

These views were particularly strong amongst current or recent learners, although substantial proportions of those who have not been engaged in learning since leaving full-time education still recognised the potential benefits of doing so (see Table 30).

Table 30. Belief in the positive impact of learning on various aspects of life, by learning status

	Total %	Current learners %	Recent learners %	Past learners %	Not since leaving full-time education %
On self confidence	86	90	91	89	79
On career/ employment prospects	83	90	90	87	74
On your child's education	75	75	77	80	71
On your health	62	66	64	64	58
On family relationships	61	61	61	64	59
On involvement in local events and issues	53	58	53	54	49
Weighted base	4,957	1,004	911	1,127	1,914

Base: all respondents

Location of, and sources of information about, learning

Twenty-eight per cent of current or recent learners say that they are learning through work; 24 per cent through university or a higher education institute; 16 per cent through a further education, tertiary or sixth form college; 12 per cent independently; 7 per cent online; 6 per cent in adult education centres or the Workers' Education Association (WEA), and 8 per cent in other venues such as schools, voluntary or community organisations or health and leisure clubs.

Men are significantly more likely than women to be learning through work, online, or independently on their own. Women are more likely to be learning at university or in community venues. As illustrated by Figure 12 below, location of learning also varies considerably by age.

Figure 12. Location of learning, by age, 2011

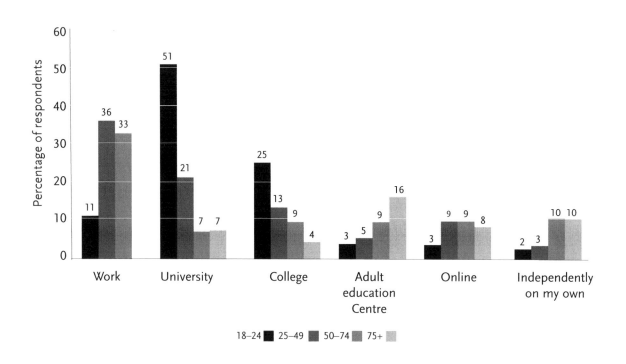

Base: all current or recent learners

When asked about the first place that they would go to find out about learning opportunities, the most popular source of information cited by those who said that they were likely to take up learning in the next three years was the Internet (43 per cent). Twelve per cent said that they would approach their local college and a further 12 per cent said they would contact a university or higher education institution. Both of these options were popular among young adults, with those aged 55 and over more likely to seek information from their local library or adult education centre (see Table 31).

As part of the 2002 survey, this same question was asked of current or recent learners. Although we need to be alive to the lack of exact comparability due to the different bases used in each year, it is apparent that over the past decade there has been a striking change in the first source of information about learning opportunities for adults. The workplace and friends and family have been displaced by the rise of the Internet.

Forty-three per cent of respondents cited the Internet as being their first place of contact, compared with just 2 per cent in 2002. Even among adults without regular access to the Internet, 11 per cent would choose the Internet first as a source of information about learning. Reliance on the Internet declines with age, with just 36 per cent of 55–64s, 22 per cent of 65–74s and 12 per cent of adults aged 75+ making the Internet their first choice for information.

Colleges and adult education centres maintain their share of first choices, universities and libraries strengthen theirs, but the collapse of reliance on managers and colleagues at work, or on family and friends outside the labour market are a real surprise.

Table 31. Sources of information about learning, by gender, 2002 and 2011 compared

	2002 All %	2002 Men %	Women %	2011 All %	2011 Men %	Women %
Workplace	33	37	29	8	9	7
Friends and family	13	12	15	2	2	2
Further education college/ tertiary/ 6th form college	11	10	11	12	11	13
University/ higher education institute	7	8	6	12	11	13
School	7	5	8	1	2	1
Adult education centre/ WEA	4	3	4	4	3	4
Internet	2	4	1	43	45	41
Library	2	2	2	5	4	5
Job Centre	2	3	1	3	3	3
Careers advice service	2	1	2	2	2	3
Weighted base	2,073	1,015	1,059	1,976	880	1,095

Base: 2002 – all current or recent learners; 2011 – all likely to take up learning in the next three years